# In the Footsteps of Explorers

# Marco Polo

## Overland to China

## Alexander Zelenyj

 Crabtree Publishing Company

www.crabtreebooks.com

# Crabtree Publishing Company

www.crabtreebooks.com

*This book is dedicated to my mother,
another world traveler with tales to tell.*

**Coordinating editor:** Ellen Rodger
**Series editor:** Carrie Gleason
**Project editor:** Adrianna Morganelli
**Editors:** Rachel Eagen, L. Michelle Nielsen
**Design and production coordinator:** Rosie Gowsell
**Cover design and production assistance:** Samara Parent
**Art direction:** Rob MacGregor
**Scanning technician:** Arlene Arch-Wilson
**Photo research:** Allison Napier

**Consultants:** Stacy Hasselbacher and Tracey L. Neikirk, The Mariners' Museum, Newport News, Virginia

**Photo Credits:** Erich Lessing/Art Resource, NY: p. 31 (right); Bibliotheque des Arts Decoratifs, Paris, France, Archives Charmet/Bridgeman Art Library: p. 24 (bottom); Bibliotheque Nationale, Paris, France, Archives Charmet/Bridgeman Art Library: p. 6 (top), p. 23 (bottom); Bibliotheque Nationale, Paris, France/Bridgeman Art Library: p. 5, p. 8, pp. 18-19, p. 22, p. 24 (top), p. 26; Bibliotheque Nationale, Paris, France, Index/Bridgeman Art Library: p. 28 (bottom); British Library, London, UK/Bridgeman Art Library: cover, p. 7 (top), pp. 8-9, p. 11 (bottom); The Great Wall, China/Bridgeman Art Library:

pp. 30-31; Private Collection/Bridgeman Art Library: pp. 6-7 (bottom), p. 25, p. 27, p. 29; Steve Bein/Corbis: p. 12 (right); Bettmann/Corbis: p. 20 (top); Christie's Images/Corbis: p. 14 (middle); Dean Conger/Corbis: pp. 12-13; Setboun/Corbis: p. 23 (top); Brian A. Vikander/Corbis: p. 11 (top); Ron Watts/Corbis: pp. 16-17; SSPL/The Image Works: p. 21 (top); Joyce Photographics/Photo Researchers, Inc.: p. 14 (bottom); Other images from stock cd

**Illustrations:** Lauren Fast: p. 4; David Wysotski: pp. 20-21

**Cartography:** Jim Chernishenko: title page, p. 10

**Cover:** The Catalan Atlas is a map of the world drawn in 1375. An illustration from the Catalan Atlas depicts Marco Polo traveling with his father Niccolo and uncle Maffeo by camel caravan in Asia.

**Title page:** Marco Polo sailed from Venice, Italy, and explored many parts of Asia, including China, India, and the Persian Gulf regions.

**Sidebar icon:** The Mongols lived in round portable tents called yurts. They brought their homes with them when they traveled from place to place in search of fresh pasture for their livestock.

## Crabtree Publishing Company

www.crabtreebooks.com        1-800-387-7650

**Cataloging-in-Publication Data**
Zelenyj, Alexander.
  Marco Polo : overland to China / written by Alexander Zelenyj.
    p. cm. -- (In the footsteps of explorers)
  Includes index.
  ISBN-13: 978-0-7787-2417-9 (rlb)
  ISBN-10: 0-7787-2417-4 (rlb)
  ISBN-13: 978-0-7787-2453-7 (pb)
  ISBN-10: 0-7787-2453-0 (pb)
  1. Polo, Marco, 1254-1323?--Juvenile literature. 2. Explorers--Italy--Biography--Juvenile literature. 3. Asia--Discovery and exploration--Juvenile literature. 4. Mongols--History--Juvenile literature.
I. Title. II. Series.
  G370.P9Z45 2005
  915.04'2'092--dc22                                          2005014944
                                                                   LC

**Published in
the United States**
PMB 16A
350 Fifth Ave.
Suite 3308
New York, NY
10118

**Published
in Canada**
616 Welland Ave.
St. Catharines
Ontario, Canada
L2M 5V6

**Published in the
United Kingdom**
73 Lime Walk
Headington
Oxford
OX3 7AD
United Kingdom

**Published
in Australia**
386 Mt. Alexander Rd.
Ascot Vale (Melbourne)
VIC 3032

# Contents

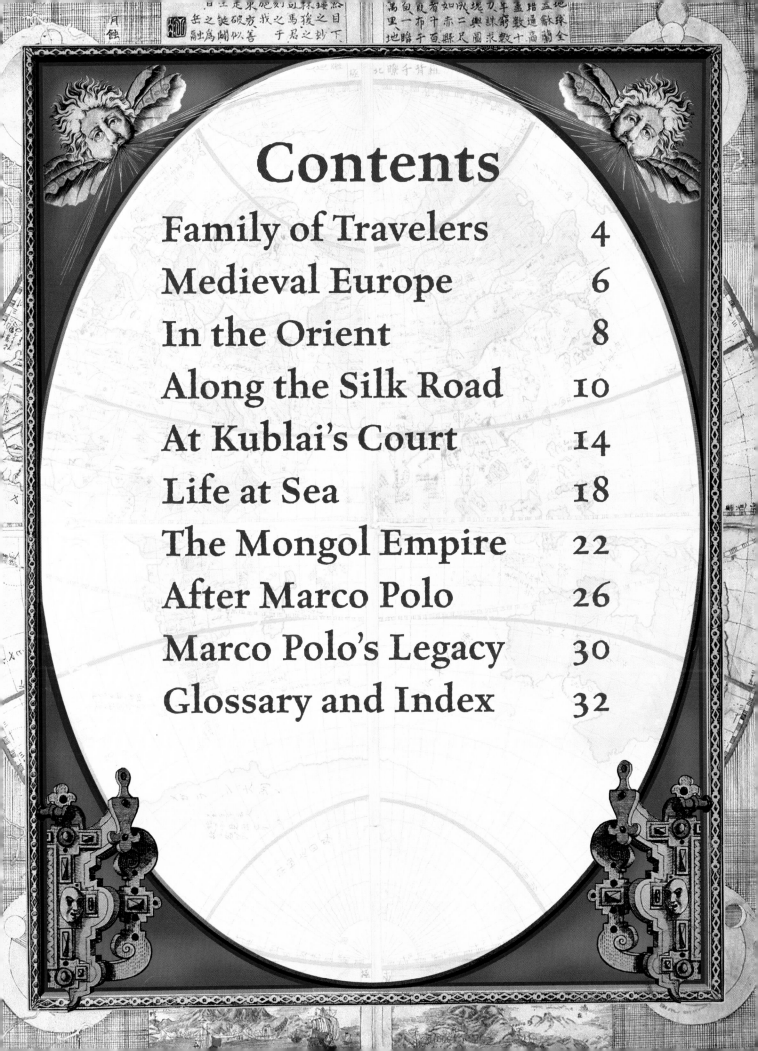

# Family of Travelers

Marco Polo was an Italian explorer who traveled to Asia, where he served in the court of China's great Mongol emperor Kublai Khan. By writing a book of his discoveries and adventures, Marco offered Europe its first look at eastern cultures and traditions.

## Explorer of Asia

When Marco Polo was 17 years old, he traveled with his father, Niccolo, and uncle, Maffeo, to Asia to meet with Kublai Khan. Marco worked in Kublai Khan's service for 17 years, traveling on missions as his official ambassador, or representative. Marco's explorations of many parts of Asia, such as China, India, and the Persian Gulf regions, and his tales of the gold, silks, and spices that he found there prompted other explorers to embark on journeys to the Far East.

## Polo's Early Life

Some historians believe Marco Polo was born into a wealthy family of merchants in the **city-state** of Venice, Italy. Before Marco was born, his father Niccolo traveled to Asia to trade grain, iron, wood, salted meat, and woven goods. Marco's mother died in 1269 before Niccolo returned home to Venice. As a boy, Marco did not receive a formal education, but he did learn to read and write Italian. Some historians believe that he gained a great deal of knowledge from the sailors he met at the wharves, or docks, who shared with him stories of distant and wondrous places.

*(above) Marco Polo was named for Saint Mark, the patron saint, or protector, of Venice.*

## Marco Polo's Journals

When Marco returned to Venice, he wrote a book of his adventures in 1298 with the help of a writer named Rusticello of Pisa. His book, *Description of the World*, was widely read by people of Europe, but many did not believe Marco's accounts because they sounded very strange and unreal.

> "They have wild elephants and plenty of unicorns, which are scarcely smaller than elephants. They have the hair of a buffalo and feet like an elephant's. They have a single large, black horn in the middle of the forehead. They do not attack with their horn, but only with their tongue and their knees; for their tongues are furnished with long, sharp spines, so that when they want to do any harm to anyone they first crush him by kneeling upon him and then lacerate him with their tongues. They have a head like a wild boar's and always carry it stooped towards the ground."

- 1254 -
Marco Polo is born in Venice, Italy.

- 1271 -
Marco Polo departs Italy for the Orient with Niccolo and Maffeo Polo.

- January 9, 1324 -
Marco Polo dies.

# Medieval Europe

The Polos traveled to Asia during the Medieval period, or the Middle Ages, a period of time that stretched from 500 A.D. to 1500 A. D. During this time, exploration was difficult and Europeans knew very little of other countries in the world.

### Venice Seaport

During the 1200s, Venice was an important seaport that lay between Asia and Europe on the Mediterranean Sea. The seaport offered traders and merchants the easiest route by water to countries in Southwest Asia and Northeast Africa. Venice's trade flourished, and slaves from Russia, Africa, and Turkey were brought there and sold, making Venice wealthy.

*(above) During the Middle Ages, many Europeans knew so little of Asia that they believed stories that the people there had heads like dogs.*

6

## Trade Wars

In 1253, the city-states of Genoa and Venice became involved in a series of wars for control of the Mediterranean Sea and the trade routes to Asia. The wars made travel by sea for exploration or trade unsafe. A peace treaty signed in 1381 finally ended the wars and Venice was declared the winner.

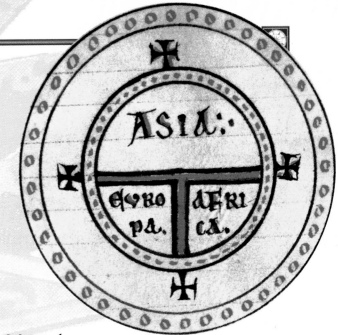

## Mongol Relations

In the 1200s, Europe's greatest enemies were the Mongols, a people from Mongolia, an area north of China. Mongol leaders wanted to **conquer** all of Europe. Groups of Mongols under many leaders attacked and ransacked European cities and villages. In 1206, a Mongol ruler named Genghis Khan united all the Mongol tribes and conquered northern China. By the time Genghis' grandson, Kublai, became Khan, or ruler, in 1260, the Mongol **empire** covered most of eastern Europe. Kublai Khan wanted peaceful relations with Europe in order to encourage trade and to learn about European culture and technology. The years between 1200 and 1300 are known as Pax Mongolica, which means "the Peace of the Mongols." Under Mongol law, no traveler could be harmed while in Mongol lands, under penalty of death. Venetian merchants traveled along the Silk Road, a series of trade routes that connected Asian and European trading centers. They traded with the Mongols for medicines, spices, perfumes, cottons, silks, and pearls.

*(above) Early medieval maps were circular, and Asia was shown to be the largest continent, filling the upper half. The arms of the T represent the Don and Nile Rivers and the middle portion was the Mediterranean Sea. Europe lay on the left side and Africa was on the right.*

*(below) Europeans referred to the Mongols as the Tartars, because they said that they came from Tartarus, or Hell.*

# In the Orient

Marco's father, Niccolo, and his uncle, Maffeo, traveled to the Orient to trade their goods. There, they met the great Mongol emperor, Kublai Khan.

## Trading in the Orient

In 1253, Niccolo and Maffeo Polo set sail from Venice, Italy, with a convoy of ships to trade iron, salted meat, and grain in Constantinople, in present-day Turkey. They traveled southeast through the Adriatic Sea past the Greek Islands and into the Sea of Marmora. After trading for six years in Constantinople, the Polos sailed to the town of Sudak in present-day Ukraine. They then traveled to the towns of Surai and Bolgara in present-day Russia. They traded for Chinese silk in Bukhoro, in Uzbekistan, and were forced to stay there for three years because a **civil war** blocked their route home to Venice.

*(below) To ensure the Polos' safe travel through Mongol lands, Kublai Khan gave them a golden tablet called a paizah, which means "tablets of command." The tablet bore the Great Khan's seal and contained the following words: "By the strength of the eternal heaven, holy be the Khan's name. Let anyone who does not pay him reverence be killed."*

## A Promise to the Great Khan

While in Bukhoro, the Polos were visited by Kublai Khan's ambassador with a message that he wished to meet them. They crossed the desert of Dzungaria and reached Kublai's palace in Khanbalik, or present-day Beijing, China. Kublai Khan asked the Polos to describe Europe's countries, rulers, and **Christianity**, which was the main religion of Europe during the Middle Ages. Before allowing them to leave, he made them promise to return with 100 experts on Christianity and a message from the Pope, or the leader of the **Roman Catholic Church**. He also asked for some holy oil from the lamp at **Jesus'** tomb in Jerusalem, which Europeans believed cured diseases of the body and soul.

## A Long Wait

The Polos spent three years traveling on foot and horseback across Asia. When they reached Armenia, they sailed to Acre, which is in present-day Syria, where they learned that Pope Clement IV had died. Forced to wait for a new Pope to be elected, the Polos worried about their lengthy absence from Kublai Khan. In 1271, newly elected Pope Gregory X granted them permission to retrieve some holy oil, and gave them gifts of crystal vases and jewelry for the Khan. The Pope presented them with two **friars**, as he was reluctant to send 100 people on such a dangerous journey. Niccolo allowed 17-year-old Marco to accompany them on their trip back to Cathay, or present-day China.

*(below) Niccolo and Maffeo Polo traveled to the Orient to trade for exotic goods such as pearls.*

- 1253 -
Niccolo and Maffeo Polo depart from Venice, Italy.

- 1266 -
Niccolo and Maffeo meet Kublai Khan.

- 1269 -
The Polo brothers return to Venice, Italy.

# Along the Silk Road

During their three-year journey to Asia, the Polos traveled along a network of trade routes known as the Silk Road. The Silk Road was used by traders who brought silk, gold, and ivory from China to Europe in return for trade goods.

## The Journey Begins

The Polos departed from Acre in 1271 with the two friars and traveled through Turkey. Frightened of the Saracens, or **Muslims**, who roamed the area in search of goods to raid, the friars left the Polos and returned to Acre. The Polos continued their journey through present-day Armenia, Anatola, Georgia, and Baghdad. They joined a **caravan** of traveling merchants.

The party journeyed through the deserts of Upper Persia, in present-day Iran, which was home to **bandits**. The caravan encountered a fierce sandstorm, which Marco believed the bandits summoned by using ancient magic. When the bandits attacked them, the Polos escaped to a nearby village, but members of their caravan were killed or sold into slavery.

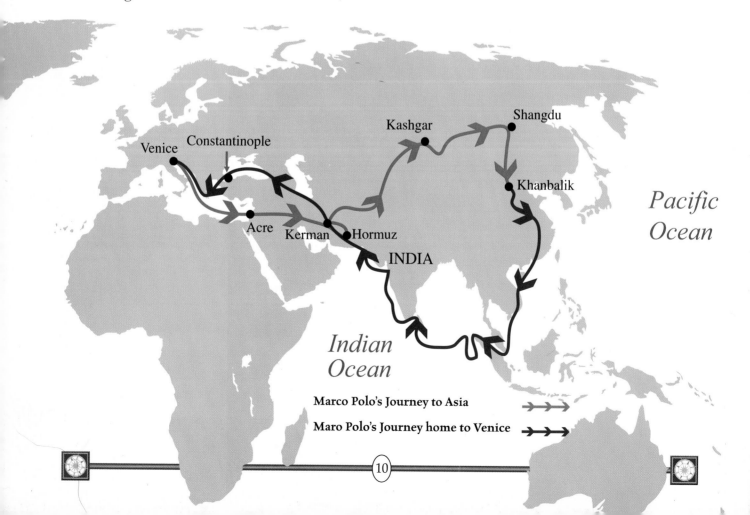

Marco Polo's Journey to Asia

Maro Polo's Journey home to Venice

## Hormuz

The Polos traveled along the **plateau** of Iran into the city of Hormuz on an island in the present-day Persian Gulf. The winds in Hormuz were so hot that people submerged themselves in water until they passed. The people of Hormuz offered the Polos ships for the rest of their journey. The ships were made of wooden boards held together with coconut yarn wound around pegs. Marco believed the ships were not seaworthy, and decided to continue on land. The Polos crossed a salt desert in eastern Iran called the Dasht-e-Lut and reached the province of Khorasan.

*(above) Caravansaries were inns that surrounded large courtyards along the Silk Road. There, traveling merchants slept, washed, ate, and received food and water for their horses and camels.*

*(background) Along the Silk Road, Afghan, Indian, and Turkish bandits often robbed travelers of their jewels, spices, silks, and incense, or forced them to pay a toll in order to pass through their lands. For protection, merchants journeyed together in large caravans.*

## Rubies and Sapphires

The Polos entered the cold region of Badakshan, in present-day Afghanistan, where people mined rubies, **lapis lazuli**, and sapphires. Marco fell ill and traveled to the Pamir Mountains in South-Central Asia, where the pure air cured him. The Polos then crossed the Pamirs, which took them 52 days. Marco observed that the shortage of oxygen high up in the mountains caused fires to burn less brightly, food not to cook as well, and kept birds from flying there. They saw a few hunters, and animal pens made of the large horns of wild sheep.

## The Trading Cities of Turkestan

After descending the Pamir Mountains, the Polos entered the plain of Chinese Turkestan, in the present-day province of Xinjiang in China. They stopped at many trading cities, such as Kashgar, where they traded for cotton cloth. In the city of Yarkand, Marco saw people suffering from **goiter**, which he thought was caused by drinking dirty water. While in Khotan in present-day Xinjiang Uygur in China, Marco noted the city's many farms, vineyards, and gardens of wheat, rice, and apricots. He also saw men digging for the gemstone jade in dried river beds.

*(right) On long journeys, merchants rode the two-humped Bactrian camel, which was strong enough to carry up to 500 pounds (227 kilograms) of merchandise. These camels have bushy eyebrows, two rows of long eyelashes, hair-lined ears, and nostrils that opened and closed, which protected them from blowing sand.*

## The Last Stretch

The Polos' last stretch of travel took them across the hot Gobi Desert, which the Chinese called the Flowing Sands. There were water wells along the way, but no food available so they had to pack many provisions, or supplies. They emerged from the desert after about a month, and arrived in Sachow, or present-day Dunhuang in China. Sachow was known as the City of Sands. While the Polos traded in Kanchow, they were met by Kublai Khan's messengers who escorted them to the Khan's summer palace in Shangdu. There, Kublai Khan greeted the Polos with a great feast.

*(background) The Polos heard stories that mirages of distant oases and traveling caravans appeared in the Gobi Desert. These mirages lured wary travelers from their routes and caused them to become lost. At night, travelers reported the eerie sounds of drums and howling.*

## Bazaars

Many trading posts, or bazaars, were located in cities along the Silk Road, where caravans traded for fresh animals, supplies, and goods. Merchants sold many Chinese goods from covered stalls and tents. The goods included cinnamon bark, rhubarb, furs, tea, ceramics, bronze weapons, belt buckles, and mirrors.

# At Kublai's Court

The Polos spent the next 17 years at Kublai Khan's court. Kublai Khan made Marco his attendant of honor and sent him on missions throughout Asia to the countries of China, India, and Burma, or present-day Myanmar.

## Kublai's Test

While at Shangdu, Kublai Khan sent Marco to the city of Karazan in eastern Persia to deliver messages from the Khan's court, and to report on all he saw in the city. Kublai Khan believed Marco to be more trustworthy than his other subjects, who were peoples the Mongols conquered and forced to be servants. When Marco returned, Kublai Khan was impressed with his report because it was more detailed than those of past messengers. Kublai Khan named Marco regional ambassador, which meant that he was to represent Kublai Khan in all lands, and to provide him with reports during all of his travels.

*(above and left) While in China, Marco saw for the first time, people using silkworms to make silk. The Chinese fed mulberry leaves to the silkworms. When the silkworms spun cocoons, the Chinese boiled the cocoons to loosen the fibres. Then they spun the fibres on a spool and wove them into silk.*

## City of 12,000 Bridges

Of all the cities Marco visited, his favorite was Kinsai, which is present-day Hangzhou in eastern China. He referred to the city as paradise, and marveled at its 3,000 public baths and 12,000 bridges. The bridges allowed Arab and Persian trading ships to enter and leave the city. There were 12 tradesmens' guilds, or groups, in Kinsai dedicated to practicing crafts such as tool-making and woodworking. Each guild had 12,000 buildings made up of 30 to 40 workers in each. Marco reported that the people of Kinsai were naturally peaceful and kept no weapons. They used small boats for leisurely sailing in the lake, and built **pavilions** for celebrations on the two islands beside the city.

## Danger in Tibet

Marco reported that many people had fled from Tibet because the country was overrun with wild tigers and other dangerous animals. Merchants and travelers protected themselves from the animals by tying large bamboo canes together and placing them around their camps. Then they lit fires around the cane bundles causing them to explode. The loud sound frightened the animals away.

- 1273 -
The Mongols conquer Siang-Yang Fou.

- 1275 -
The Polos reach Asia.

- 1292 -
The Polos escort Princess Kocachin to Persia.

- 1294 -
Kublai Khan dies.

- 1295 -
The Polos return to Venice, Italy.

## Tomb of Gold

Marco reported that the people of Burma covered their teeth with gold, and men tattooed striped patterns around their arms and legs. They used elephants for riding into battle against the Mongols. In the city of Mien, Marco saw the tomb of a king made of gold and silver **pagodas**. He wrote that he saw magicians and oxen as tall as elephants in the province of Bangala, present-day Bangladesh, and met a king with 400 wives in the country of Kangigu, present-day Mayanmar.

## Niccolo and Maffeo's Services

Marco's reports claim that Niccolo and Maffeo were military advisors for the Mongols. They helped the Khan conquer the town of Siang-Yang Fou in China by teaching the Mongols how to build **mangonels** for the battle. Historians today question Marco's report because historical records show that Siang-Yang Fou fell to Kublai Khan two years before the Polos arrived in Asia. Many believe that Niccolo and Maffeo remained at Kublai's court, trading to build their fortunes, and that they did not teach the Mongols how to do battle.

*(background) In his reports, Marco Polo claimed to have been governor of the city of Yangzhou, in China, from 1282 to 1285. There are no historical reports that show any record of this. Some historians believe that Marco only visited the city as an ambassador bringing messages from the Mongol Emperor. Others believe that he served there for three years as a tax inspector for the Privy Council, or council that advised the Khan.*

## Homesick

In 1291, the Polos decided to return home to Venice. Kublai Khan was now 76 years old, and the Polos were worried about their safety if the Khan were to die because many Mongols were jealous of the Khan's treatment of the Polos. The Khan would not allow the Polos to leave because he had grown fond of them. Soon after, three messengers from Persia visited Kublai Khan with news that the wife of Argon, the Khan of Persia, had died. Her dying wish was for Kublai to choose a Mongolian bride for Argon, and he chose a princess named Kocachin. The messengers asked Kublai Khan to allow Marco to escort them overseas to Persia, and Kublai Khan consented. He also allowed the Polos to visit their families in Venice, but made them promise to return.

## Homeward Bound

The Polos sailed from China with a fleet of 14 ships supplied by Kublai Khan. They sailed for more than two years, until they reached Hormuz on the Persian Gulf. After escorting the princess, they rested from their journey in Tabriz, Iran, where they received news that Kublai Khan had died. The Polos finally reached Venice in 1295.

*(below) While in Karazan in eastern Persia, Marco encountered strange and terrible animals, which he compared to huge serpents. These were actually crocodiles, and Marco learned that hunters used their gall to treat people who had been bitten by rabid animals.*

# Life at Sea

During the 1200s, overseas journeys were long and difficult. Crew members were faced with many dangers, such as storms, diminishing food and supplies, and attacks from pirates who robbed ships and murdered their crews.

(background) The Polos used a device called an astrolabe to measure the *altitude* of the sun or stars. The ship's position was determined by focusing on a known star.

**- Dead Reckoning -**

The position of the ship was calculated by measuring the course and distance sailed from a known point.

**- Celestial Navigation -**

Judging the ship's position based on the sun or the stars is called celestial navigation.

### The Ships

Historians are not certain what type of ship the Polos used to sail home to Italy from Asia. Some believe they sailed in a large, fast ship called a galley. Galleys were long and narrow and were powered by oars, and sometimes sails. During the Middle Ages, galleys were armed with weapons and a crew of rowers and were used as warships. Merchants also sailed in galleys laden with goods to trade in other countries.

(above) *During the Middle Ages, many sailors believed that whales were deadly sea monsters. In his book, Marco described the severe damage that whales caused to ships at sea.*

(below) *Many people wrongly believed that Marco Polo discovered macaroni and ice cream in China and introduced them to Europe when he returned to Italy. In his book, Marco compared a type of pasta eaten by the Chinese to lasagna or macaroni. He also wrote of a form of dried milk that the Mongols ate for energy before battle.*

# Millet

While in Asia, Marco Polo found that the Mongols often used millet in their cooking. Millet is a small grain that has a mild flavor. Here's how you can make your own millet:

1 cup (250 mL) millet
2 cups (500 mL) water
1 tsp (5 mL) olive oil
1/4 tsp (1 mL) salt

1. Rinse the millet and drain in a strainer.
2. Put millet in a saucepan with the water, olive oil, and salt, and bring to a boil.
3. Reduce the heat, and cover the saucepan with the lid. Let it simmer for about 20 minutes or until all the water is absorbed.
4. Turn off the heat and let it sit for five minutes.
5. Fluff the millet with a fork. Enjoy.

## Hardships

Aboard ship, rats and cockroaches swarmed everywhere, and the smell of **bilge water** and rotting wood made it difficult to breathe. Sailors ate meat and fish that were dried and salted so that they would not spoil. They also ate a type of biscuit called hardtack, cheese, vinegar, garlic, and onions. Many sailors died from illnesses, such as scurvy, which was a common disease caused by a lack of vitamin C found in fresh fruits and vegetables. The captain of the ship slept in his own cabin, but the crew had to sleep on deck, or in the ship's hold, the area below deck, among the food and other supplies

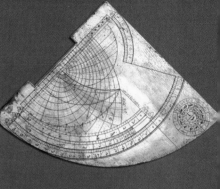

*(background) Ship's boys were responsible for keeping track of time, cooking and serving hot meals to the sailors, leading morning prayers, and scrubbing the decks.*

*(left) Cockroaches, weevils, and rats often infested the ship's food supplies.*

## - Quadrant -

A quadrant was a device used to determine a ship's latitude, or how far north or south it was. One arm of the instrument was aligned with the horizon and the other arm was aligned with the sun or stars. The greater the angle, the further the ship was from the equator, or the imaginary belt around the center of the Earth.

# The Mongol Empire

The Mongols' vast empire stretched from Southeast Asia to Eastern Europe. When Kublai Khan conquered northern China in 1271, China became part of his empire and influenced the Mongolian way of life.

*(above) The Mongol cavalry was made up of archers and swordsmen on horseback. Mongol warriors were gifted horsemen who moved quicker than their enemies did on foot.*

## Mongol Government

Mongol tribes were led by a king called a khan. The khan was elected by the tribe leaders at gatherings called *khuriltais*. The Mongol empire consisted of a committee of leaders called *kurultai*, who met with the khan to discuss issues involving Mongol lands, and to ensure that tribes were not fighting one another. The Mongols were governed by a code of law called *yasa*, and penalties for not obeying the laws were severe, including death.

## Mongol Homes

Mongol homes, called yurts, were round tents made from felt and canvas tied over wooden frames. Smoke from cooking and heating fires escaped through a hole in the roof called a *shangrak*. Beaten cow or pony dung mixed with sand served as a foundation for the floor. Wealthy Mongol families hung felt rugs on the walls for protection against the cold during winter. In the summer, they hung screens made of reeds on yurt walls to keep out dust and insects. Yurts had no windows, and the door was made of a felt flap.

## Learning from the Chinese

After becoming the emperor of China in 1260, Kublai Khan learned of many Chinese technologies. He learned how to extract **asbestos** from rock to produce candle wicks and cloth. The Mongols used coal to produce fire after seeing the Chinese heat their baths with it, and adopted the Chinese use of paper money instead of gold and silver coins. Kublai Khan also borrowed a message delivery system from the Chinese called the Imperial Post. Messengers carried mail over long distances on horseback, and stopped at stations called yambs every 25 to 30 miles (40 to 48 kilometers) to stock up on food and water. Stations were also located every three miles (4.8 kilometers) for foot-runners, or messengers who traveled short distances on foot.

*(above) The accumulation of smoke stains around the shangrak's, or roof hole's, edges represented the long life of a Mongol family. When the yurt became worn and was rebuilt, the shangrak was kept and passed down from father to son.*

*(below) In his book, Marco explained that the Mongols made sheets of paper from the bark of the mulberry tree. They were cut into pieces and used as money.*

(left) Kublai Khan hunted wild game, such as bear, boar, and deer, with the help of trained falcons, cheetahs, leopards, dogs, and lynxes.

(below) Each Mongol tribe had a male shaman, or doctor, called a Boege and a female shaman called an Idugan. They drove away evil spirits, communicated with the gods, and told fortunes.

## Food

The Mongols were a **nomadic** people who moved their homes from place to place in search of food, water, and grazing land for their cattle. Meat was an important part of their diet. They hunted deer and caught mice and rats. They cooked meat over fires fueled by horse or cow dung and wood, or they ate it raw. During the summer, the Mongols ate leeks, wild onions, hazelnuts, and fruits such as juniper berries, wild apples, and cherries. They drank fermented mare and camel milk called *koumiss*, and used the milk to make curds, yogurt, and cheese.

## Roles

Mongol women made felt, cooked, raised the children, and sewed clothing, shoes, and bags from animal hides. They were trained to use weapons to defend their herds of cattle from predatory animals. Women were respected in Mongol society, and were able to inherit property and divorce their husbands. Most Mongol men were warriors skillfully trained to use bows and arrows, swords, and knives. Mongol boys were taught to ride horses in preparation for future battles.

## Mongol Beliefs and Religion

The Mongols believed in many gods that they prayed to for help and approval. Their Supreme Being was a sky-god named Everlasting Blue Sky, who ruled over nature deities, or gods of the natural world. They often made animal **sacrifices** to their gods at mounds of stones and on top of hills. The Mongols placed **idols** of their gods, made of silk and felt, in carts outside their yurts to protect their homes. They also hung idols over the beds of the sick to cure them. When they killed an animal, they offered its heart to the idols.

## Chinese Junks

The Mongols sailed in large Chinese ships called junks. Most junks were made of teak wood. Each junk had three to five masts and a curved sail framed with bamboo poles, which propelled the ships and allowed them to sail very fast. Junks required a crew of about 300, and some had sweeps, or oars, each manned by four seamen. They were built with many water-tight **bulkheads** that protected the ship from sinking if it hit a rock or was struck by a whale. Some junks had up to 60 cabins below the deck, which had sleeping quarters and compartments to store food and other goods.

*(below) For the Polos' trip home, Kublai Khan prepared a fleet of 14 Chinese junks stocked with provisions to last for two years.*

# After Marco Polo

Nobody would ever know Marco Polo's fantastic tales of adventure and exploration if Marco had not returned to Italy and written a book. There are many myths about the voyage, and some of them were invented by Marco himself.

## Welcome Home

A popular legend tells that upon returning to Italy and presenting themselves to their relatives, the Polos were not recognized at all. They were dressed in clothes that were soiled and tattered from their voyage, and they had aged since they had embarked on their journey to the Orient 25 years earlier. The Polos tore open their robes to reveal the precious jewels they had hidden. Their family then believed their story and welcomed them back into the family.

*(below) At first, Kublai Khan was reluctant to allow the Polos to leave his empire. He only consented when they promised to return. Marco Polo was 17 years old when he left Venice and 41 when he returned.*

## Imprisoned!

In 1296, Marco joined the Venetian army in a battle against Genoa for control of the Mediterranean Sea as a trade route. During a battle near the island of Curzola in the Adriatic Sea, he was captured by the Genoans and put in prison. There, he met a fellow prisoner named Rustichello of Pisa. For the next three years, Rustichello and Marco wrote a book of Marco's adventures in Asia entitled *Description of the World*. Marco was set free from prison in 1299, when Genoa and Venice signed a peace treaty.

## Marco il Milione

Many Europeans who read Marco's book believed it was full of lies. Marco and his book became nicknamed Marco il Milione, or Marco Millions, because it was said that Marco was a man with a million invented stories. To other Europeans, Marco's accounts of the peoples of the East showed that they were alike in many ways.

*(above) Rustichello was a writer who enjoyed Marco's stories of his adventures in Asia. For three years, he and Marco set down the Polos' adventures on paper.*

- 1295 -
**The Polos return home to Venice, Italy.**

- 1296 -
**Marco Polo is imprisoned in Genoa, Italy.**

- 1298 -
**Marco Polo and Rustichello write *Description of the World*.**

- 1299 -
**Venice and Genoa sign a peace treaty.**

- 1325 -
Muslim explorer
Ibn Battuta
travels in Asia
and Africa for
30 years.

- 1492 -
Italian explorer
Christopher
Columbus
(above) sails the
Atlantic Ocean
and reaches
America, which
he believes to
be Asia.

- 1570s -
Explorer Martin
Frobisher
searches
unsuccessfully
for a sea passage
from Europe to
the Orient.

## The Age of Exploration

Marco Polo carried word of China's scientific and cultural advances back to Europe. His tales of the great wealth to be found in Asia inspired other Europeans to travel outside of Europe. Merchants and explorers ventured to China, India, and the Moluccas, or Spice Islands, in search of valuable trade goods, such as silk, gold, and spices, including pepper, cinnamon, and cloves.

*(above right) Europeans sailed to Asia for valuable spices. In Europe, spices were used to make medicines and hide the taste of salted meat.*

*(right) The Catalan Atlas is a map of the world drawn in 1375 that illustrates Marco Polo's ideas about the geography of Asia. Illustrations based on his stories decorate the map.*

## The Mongols

In the years following the Polos' stay in Asia, the Mongol empire crumbled. Many Chinese resented the Mongol emperors. In 1368, a **Buddhist** scholar named Ming T'ai Tsu organized an army and forced the Mongols from China. Ming T'ai Tsu rose to the throne to become the first ruler of the Ming **dynasty**. The Mongols were completely expelled from China by 1382, ending the reign of the largest empire the world had ever seen.

*(below) Once driven out of China, the Mongols continued to harass the Chinese, but were unable to reconquer China.*

# Marco Polo's Legacy

Marco Polo's book continues to be read today, and his adventures have made him one of the most important and famous travelers in history.

## Marco's Controversial Book

Today, many historians believe that much of Marco Polo's book, *Description of the World,* is untrue, and that he did not visit China. This is because he failed to mention important features of China, such as the Great Wall, tea, Chinese **calligraphy** and writing, chopsticks, or the binding of women's feet. Marco also did not use Chinese words in his book, but used Mongol and Turkish words instead. Other historians argue that Marco's omissions can be explained, and that his detailed descriptions of China's currency, Imperial Post, and use of silkworms and coal prove that he had been there.

*(below) While in Badakshan, Marco Polo saw large-horned wild sheep, which were named Ovis Poli, or Marco Polo's sheep, in his honor.*

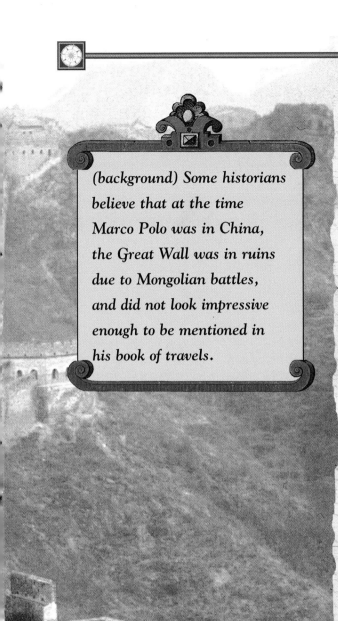

(background) Some historians believe that at the time Marco Polo was in China, the Great Wall was in ruins due to Mongolian battles, and did not look impressive enough to be mentioned in his book of travels.

## Polo's Writings

The information on events and people in this book are based on Marco Polo's writings. Today, some historians question the facts presented in his reports.

## Artwork

There were no cameras or video recording equipment during the Medieval period. The artwork in this book was created later by artists who were not present at the events. For this reason, the events may not have happened exactly as they appear in this book, but in styles that were popular during an artist's lifetime.

(right) One legend says that on his deathbed, a priest asked Marco Polo whether he wanted to admit that some of his stories were untrue. Marco answered, "I did not tell half of what I saw, for I knew I would not be believed."

# Glossary

**altitude** The height of something from sea level or the Earth's surface

**asbestos** A mineral that separates into fibres and can be woven to make fireproof material

**bandit** A group of robbers

**bilge water** Water that collects in the bilge, or lower portion of a ship's hull

**Buddhism** A religion founded by Buddha, an ancient religious leader from India

**bulkhead** A dividing wall between compartments on a ship

**calligraphy** The art of fine handwriting

**caravan** A group of travelers journeying together, often for safety reasons

**Christianity** A religion based on the teachings of Jesus Christ, whom Christians believe is the son of God

**city-state** A region controlled by a city

**civil war** A war between people of the same land

**conquer** To take over by force

**court** A pharaoh or a king and all those around him, including his family, personal servants, advisors, and officials

**dynasty** A succession of rulers of the same family

**empire** One political unit that occupies a large region of land and is governed by one ruler

**friar** A member of a group of Christian men

**gall** An organ inside an animal's body

**goiter** An enlargement of the thyroid gland that causes swelling of the neck

**harass** To attack or bother over and over again

**idol** An object that is worshiped as a god

**Jesus** A man who Christians believe preached the word of God and healed people

**lapis lazuli** A blue semiprecious gemstone

**mangonel** A device used to hurl heavy objects, such as boulders

**Mongol** People from a region north of China

**Muslims** Followers of Islam. Muslims believe in one god, Allah, and follow the teachings of the prophet Muhammad

**nomadic** Traveling from place to place for food

**oasis** An area in a desert where plants grow because there is water

**pagoda** A Buddhist religious building

**pavilion** A large tent

**plateau** An area of flat land that is higher than the surrounding land

**rabid** Having the fatal disease, rabies, which causes convulsions and madness

**Roman Catholic Church** A branch of Christianity that focuses on traditional religious beliefs, practices, and rituals

**sacrifice** A religious ceremony in which a human being or an animal is killed and offered to a god or a goddess

# Index

1 2 3 4 5 6 7 8 9 0 Printed in the U.S.A. 4 3 2 1 0 9 8 7 6 5